A Smart Start for Professional Development

From Sticky Notes to Dragon Boats

20 Slightly Off-Kilter Activities for Middle Schools

A Smart Start for Professional Development

From Sticky Notes
to
Dragon Boats

20 Slightly Off-Kilter Activities for Middle Schools

Jan Burgess

NATIONAL MIDDLE SCHOOL ASSOCIATION
Westerville, Ohio

Printed in the United States of America.

Betty Edwards, Executive Director
Jeff Ward, Deputy Executive Director
April Tibbles, Director of Publications
Edward Brazee, Editor, Professional Publications
John Lounsbury, Consulting Editor, Professional Publications
Mary Mitchell, Designer, Editorial Assistant
Dawn Williams, Publications Manager
Nikia Reveal, Graphic Designer
Dina Cooper, Graphic Designer
Marcia Meade-Hurst, Senior Publications Representative
Peggy Rajala, Publications Marketing/Ad Sales Coordinator

Library of Congress Cataloging-in-Publication Data
Burgess, Jan.
 A smart start for professional development: sticky notes to dragon boats: 20 slightly off-kilter activities for middle schools/by Jan Burgess.
    p. cm.
 Includes bibliographical references.
 ISBN 978-1-56090-217-1
 1. Middle school principals--United States. 2. Educational leadership--United States. 3. Teacher effectiveness--United States. I. Title
LB2822.2.B87 2008
373.12' 012--dc22

                                        2007047800

National Middle School Association
4151 Executive Parkway, Suite 300
Westerville, Ohio 43081
1-800-528-NMSA f: 614-895-4750
www.nmsa.org

About the Author

 Janet B. Burgess retired as principal of Lake Oswego Junior High School, Lake Oswego, Oregon, in 2004. Currently on the Board of National Middle School Association as West Region Trustee, Jan continues her professional activities advocating for effective middle schools, strong leadership teams, and the concept of the interdependence of relationships and academic achievement.

Jan consults with her husband, business partner, and best friend, Pete Lorain, on strategic planning, school improvement, and middle level theory and practice.

When not enmeshed in all things middle level, Jan pursues several activities that define her life these days, including travel to places she would like to visit before she gets too old. She is always ready to head somewhere she hasn't explored before and lose herself in the art, smells, colors, and people of other cultures.

In winter, Jan likes nothing better than to hunker down with a pile of new books, including recent young adolescent literature, and immerse herself in reading for as many days as she can get away with.

Jan and Pete stay connected with their two grown sons, daughter-in-law, and family, all of whom delight her in many ways. She hikes with a women's group, does a bit of yoga, and collects thoughts and phrases on bits of paper just in case another article or book surfaces.

Contents

List of Activities

Foreword

Every school consists of multiple components. Sometimes these components work together, sometimes they work independently of one another, and sometimes they are in conflict. In every successful school, the key is an effective principal—a leader who weaves a thread through the components and ties them together so all work toward a common goal.

This work provides innovative, creative, and hands-on ways a leader can connect the elements of a middle school, create metaphors for a school and a school year, and bring school goals to life.

Leadership is *a*—if not *the*—dominant factor in any effective school. While in every school there are excellent teachers and sound programs, a strong principal is needed to bring them together to make the school successful for staff, students, and parents. Such a principal grasps the many parts of a school, senses how they relate and interact, and views it all as a gestalt. In much the same way that a teacher creates an effective classroom, the strong principal operates similarly, but on a broader scale.

In this unusual resource, my wife and author Jan Burgess claims, "The framework for good teaching is also an excellent model for leaders." Here she applies that tenet to directly model a strategy as she plans and carries out activities that build a positive community. A good teaching model relates to school leadership in three other ways:

- Teachers have high expectations for all students; the principal has high expectations for all teachers, students, and school programs.

- Teachers create environments, structures, and conditions so students can learn, grow, and be successful; the principal does the same for the teachers and the entire school community.
- Teachers individualize and differentiate instruction to meet the needs of all children; the principal individualizes and differentiates to meet the needs of all staff members.

Jan used relationships and achievement as the foci for her work as a principal. These concepts provided the foundation for her thinking, her goals, and her leadership. They were the criteria against which she based all school decisions and directions, sometimes carefully and consciously, other times instinctively or somewhere in between on the continuum of decision making. Quality decisions require a leader with relationship-building skills, a belief that relationships are important, and a continual orientation to student achievement. In these two concepts, relationships and achievement, she encompasses the single most important element in effective schools or any organization (relationships) and uses it to facilitate and maximize the primary reason schools exist (student achievement).

Schools are judged to be successful in many ways: teacher efficacy, student attitudes and perceptions, parent involvement and support, relevant curriculum, individualized and differentiated instruction, and others. None of these interrelated standards is more significant than student performance and achievement. It is through effective leadership that these conditions come together to ensure success for all students.

Effective leaders hold core beliefs. They model and inspire. They have a blueprint that enables them to provide the leadership necessary to make everyone in school successful. Jan does those things, and in this book she shares many of her not-so-secret ideas and her passion.

All activities recorded here chronicle successful past experiences, if faculty feedback and yearlong applications are valid measurements for success. These activities are interesting, fun, supportive, and real. The power of the book is in this message—fresh, creative, and innovative approaches to opening the school year are not only desirable and effective but limitless in number and kind. *A Smart Start for Professional Development* promises that schooling can be original, exciting, and individually responsive—as it should be. Schools are all different, and they are different every year. It is primarily the principal who must recognize a changing environment and adjust the goals, the approaches, and the leadership of the school to match its dynamic individuality.

Many times I have observed Jan as she prepares for a school year. She begins in the spring as she sets goals with individual staff members and collaborates with her leadership team to prepare for the coming year. She thoughtfully works in the summer to prepare for an opening experience, one that will set the stage for addressing the year's goals. She identifies and secures resources for professional growth activities throughout the year. During these months I have seen her paint horseshoes, phone colleagues asking for assistance, and call the head of the parent group to seek funds for one of her adventures. These are only a few of the preparatory experiences as Jan gets an idea, develops it, and bravely and confidently crafts yet another interesting and relevant way to set the tone and the continuity thread for another year.

Enjoy this book. Use the activities as they are, or adapt them, or just let them stimulate your own imagination and creativity. Remember that it takes a dedicated and creative leader, one who believes in relationships and student achievement, to bring all elements together for a successful educational endeavor.

Pete Lorain
Lake Oswego, Oregon
January 2008

Introduction

Leadership is the most significant and necessary ingredient as a school strives to increase student achievement. An effective school must have a principal who establishes, promotes, and fosters positive relationships. When such relationships are focused on achievement, success in school improvement will result.

Summarized, this concept might be stated as a formula:

It takes the power of relationships with an achievement orientation to move a school forward.

Successful leaders understand this conceptual formula and recognize both parts as crucial for success.

- George Balanchine knew it and used the components with his ballet corps to execute breathtaking movement.
- Duke Blue Devils' coach Mike Krzyzewski and his staff based their coaching strategy and teaching on a similar formula.
- The final "Survivor" team on TV harnessed its power and gained the winning points through application of the formula.
- Investment giant Wachovia Securities has as a marketing slogan: "Together we can achieve uncommon results."

Leaders can bring this formula to life through activities, structures, and systems. The activities and simulations described in this book are designed to build context by creating situations that foster positive relationships. That way a group of individuals emerges as a single, purposeful faculty—one that works together, plans together, and shares the same vision for student and school success. These contextual experiences create metaphors for as long as a year and provide quick reference points and reminders of goals set and lessons learned. They frame ongoing discussions, investigations, and perspectives for faculty contemplation, and can be the catalyst for action.

Strong, positive relationships between and among adults and students with a focus on academic achievement provide the foundations for excellence. The lessons and stories about relationships and an achievement orientation remain the same whether told by Coach Dean Smith, former basketball coach at the University of North Carolina, or found in a recent compilation of effective schools' studies that Robert Marzano (2003) outlined in *What Works in Schools: Translating Research Into Action.* Similarly, the research literature on effective middle schools, from the Carnegie Council on Adolescent Development's report *Turning Points* (1989), and Felner's longitudinal middle grades research studies (1997), to National Middle School Association's *This We Believe in Action* (2005) highlights the critical nature of positive relationships and an achievement orientation to middle school improvement.

Regardless of the physical structure of the school or its grade configuration, just as the classroom teacher and team are responsible for building and providing the context for student learning, it is the principal who is responsible for the overall school culture. Leadership's goal should be to create relationships and structures within the school that support individual students as they achieve and grow academically.

"Leaders create the conditions for others' success," says Dr. William Korach, superintendent, Lake Oswego Public Schools, Oregon. Leaders must establish a climate of relational trust so that contentious and difficult issues are allowed to surface and be discussed. Trust grows over time, incrementally and gradually, through experiences, interactions, and exchanges. "Developing a culture of relational trust and disciplined performance is very difficult," says Anthony Alvarado, former chancellor of instruction in the San Diego City School District. "Such a culture must be guided, cultivated, and confronted" (Fullan, 2003a). It is up to the principal, as leader, to design and bring forward capacity-building strategies and experiences that support a focus on continuous improvement and that validate and accept differing voices.

Many successful leaders develop their leadership strength and support through thoughtful engagement. They ask key questions of their constituents to create a shared vision for action and create conditions for others' successes. They create a framework, design a blueprint, draw a road map, and provide a structure that others help fill in. Questions that lead such discussions include:

- What do we believe?
- Where are we going?
- How will we know when we get there?
- When is *good* good enough?
- Do we all have to get there together?
- What is the formula to move from *them* to *us*?

The research about what is important to create high-performing middle schools is clear (Carnegie Council on Adolescent Development, 1989; Felner, 1997; NMSA, 2003). The challenge is how to inspire others to examine and embrace the direction and goals that are key to a successful middle level school. How does the principal build context that inspires teachers to accept the hard work and the shared responsibility for each student's success—or, as Dean Smith (2004) noted, "play hard, play together, and play smart" (p. 30).

In my 18 years as a building principal, part of my signature was to leverage leadership with bold activities, ones that were meaning makers. I wanted the faculty and staff to "play hard, play smart, and play together" as we created a metaphor for our work. Each year we had an engaging opening school activity, which became a theme that connected our goals and work for the entire school year.

As you read about these activities, three questions will no doubt arise.

First, where did you get the ideas for these various activities and venues? Anywhere I could find them! Team-building ideas abound if you look. First I asked in the spring and summer, "How are we meeting our goals for all students?" Once I had a general theme in mind, and knowing I had limited time and in some years very limited funds, I set off to match the theme with the perfect activity. Some of the best ideas were borrowed and refined from various graduate classes colleagues told me about, things that had been carried out in some prior context and with a different group. Some came from conversations with business people about their retreats. Ideas came from our state's leadership summer camps. One activity is a variation of an exercise our school's food services coordinator designed for her staff, which was perfect for the leadership team. Simply stated, I listened, I looked, I asked questions, I mined parent club contacts, and I connected with local service clubs and neighborhood businesses. For over 18 years I kept an idea file, drawing on its contents when the time was right.

Second, what about time? All administrators face the constraint of time. Beginning-of-the-year activities are usually tightly scheduled with all-district meetings and allocated work times. My challenge was to take the opening school professional development day allotted to administration and use that one day to frame a few simple messages through an opening activity. Big, all-day faculty meetings were a thing of the past. With a bold activity to start the day (as little as 90 minutes to several hours), the rest of day one was for teams to work together. Other administrative messages were handed out on bright pink paper to be read at the staff's convenience.

Finally, what about money? Limited funds never stopped an activity or idea from blossoming. I tapped every source I could, including local service clubs, parent groups, businesses, and neighborhood stores such as the coffee shop and grocery store. I didn't just ask for a handout; we formed ongoing partnerships so both sides prospered. Teachers and students connected with these clubs and businesses for service activities; they in turn sponsored part of an activity cost. We set up a tutoring partnership with a local college, who in turn shared campus facilities at no charge. One parent, co-owner of an athletic club, was happy to let us use the facility for one major activity, as it also promoted the business. The local coffee company furnished coffee and bottles of water, while our students kept the store supplied with original art throughout the year. The school's parent club agreed to furnish lunch on the opening day—often the best lunch of the year! And, for the price of gas for a bus, a bus driver became our chauffeur to whatever location was the site for one of the opening day professional development activities.

I worked closely with the school's leadership team through the annual budget process. Each year we agreed to put aside up to $500 for professional development. This was often used to buy gas, to pay nominal fees or honorariums, or to purchase materials.

With an idea in mind and time and funding constraints resolved, I sent a formal invitation to all faculty and staff, inviting them to participate in an opening-of-school activity. Except what to wear, no specifics were given to keep the activity a surprise. Curiosity and anxiety came into play. Individuals were assured they were to participate as they felt comfortable, knowing each person had the support of the rest. Safety and comfort with the activities were always considered. The purpose of these activities was to stretch ourselves, to be "off kilter" just enough to see things in a new way; to experience success as a team; to ensure deep, rich conversations; and to move away from the traditional one-size-fits-all professional development presentation in the school library.

Bold activities became business as usual. Faculty and staff knew we would play and work hard together. We connected with each other in good times so we'd be there for each other when more difficult times came. The activity or theme became our framework, one to which we constantly referred so as to remind ourselves of the things we now saw more clearly or differently, and to remind ourselves that we were one, together for students and each other.

In every case, even as I changed schools, the year began with a vision-building activity such as those described in this book. Everyone's voice contributed to clarifying our vision, dreaming of where we wanted to be, and mapping how we'd take that journey together. I invite you to do the same.

Remember—it takes the power of relationships with an achievement orientation to move a school forward.

1. The Teaching-Leading Model

The model for good teaching provides a sound framework for leadership. It is based on the two foundations of the formula for success set forth in the introduction: relationships and a focus on achievement.

Master teachers develop a conceptual framework prior to teaching any unit of study. Knowing their students and curriculum content well, they identify key concepts they want students to understand and be able to use when the unit of study is complete. They relate the big questions of the unit to students' interests. Next, they outline the learning goals and create meaningful activities and structures that allow for student involvement (process) and results (product). They begin with the end—the learning—in mind and build backwards. To begin teaching, the master teacher creates an experience, a simulation, or an engaging activity that symbolizes the learning and threads the concepts together.

The principal can use this same framework to plan activities that will engage the faculty in building a common understanding for school improvement (success for all students). The blueprint will include the essential components of the teaching model: nurture strong relationships, focus deeply on achievement, and share the responsibility for success.

A first task is to design activities that will build context and support relationships among teachers and administrators with enough intellectual challenge to engage even the most veteran staff member. Sometimes, in order to see things anew, leaders must take their constituents outside their own comfort areas to add texture to conversations. The following activity will do that.

Building the Vision Together
(All-School Activity)

Purpose: To engage all faculty members in considering, creating, and designing the future of the school through a defined process. This affinity exercise helps identify beliefs that provide the substance as you establish your school's vision, which in turn creates the framework for your school improvement plan.

Description: This activity involves reflecting on the hopes, dreams, successes, and needs of your school. In a room with multiple tables for small groups and space for chart packs and the like, faculty groups will respond in writing to three focusing questions. These will be shared, folded in with other thoughts and ideas until all ideas, hopes, and dreams are displayed. Common themes, patterns, and outliers help narrow and condense the dialogue as a single common vision is created. Depending on the size of the group, the process can take up to two hours.

Process: Give each person several sticky notes. Then create table groups of equal numbers (four to eight) by dividing participants by birth month for variety. Emphasize that there is no talking allowed for the first part of this activity.

Pose three questions to the faculty, allowing about three minutes for individual reflection and writing for each question:

1. What are your hopes and dreams for our school?
2. What needs attention at our school?
3. How will we know our school is successful?

Individual participants write one idea, sentence, or phrase per sticky note.

Next, pair individuals at tables and have them share their answers by showing sticky notes to each other, still with no talking. Pairs combine like answers and devise labels for each set.

Now, have pairs double up and share their set of sticky notes with each other, again looking for like answers. *Talking is now allowed.* Label like categories. Then, on chart pads, each table group posts its labeled sets. Share these with another table. Look for areas of agreement and difference. Move any sticky notes that do not fit into a labeled grouping to the side and label those "singletons." Allow questions to surface as singletons are identified as such. This will spark additional conversation.

Ask each table group to choose a spokesperson to share the major labeled sets and singletons with the entire faculty. Once each group has shared, thank the participants. Record all labeled sets and share the written summaries with all participants.

As a second step in gathering ideas and insights, representatives from the school's parent groups and student leaders can also complete this visioning activity. Their responses, which highlight their perceptions of school direction, strengths, and needs, will be shared with the faculty.

Finally, reconvene as a group to consider this additional information along with recent academic achievement data. Direct that conversation by asking: "Knowing what we now know, where do we want to be three to five years from now? How will we get there?" The school's Leadership Team will take these conversations and begin drafting a school improvement plan with academic and instructional goals, school climate and culture goals, and management goals.

Materials needed: Chart paper, markers, one sticky notepad per person, tables, and chairs.

Debriefing questions:

- What are your hopes and dreams for our school?
- What works at our school?
- What needs attention at our school?
- How will we know when we are successful?

Follow-up: As the information is distilled and condensed into a vision statement for the school by the school's LeadershipTeam, this vision statement is ready to be shared and massaged further so that it represents the best thinking of the collective group.

The Leadership Team is now poised to put together an action plan that describes how each goal will be addressed on the journey to making this vision a reality. Once the school improvement plan is in place, give all faculty members and parent groups a copy. "Dipsticking"—regularly revisiting the document to refine it or refocus the school's work—is imperative to keep the vision alive. January and mid-May are both opportune times to make adjustments as the three- to five-year goals in the school improvement plan become the road map to the school's vision.

Effective professional development experiences are collaborative affairs.

2. Building Context with Opening School Activities

I n *The Moral Imperative of School Leadership*, Michael Fullan (2003b) stated, "The leader's job is to help change context—to introduce new elements into the situation that are bound to influence behavior for the better" (p. 1). Similarly, Gladwell (2000) added, "If you want to change people's beliefs and behavior you need to create a community around them, where these new beliefs could be practical, expressed, and nurtured" (p. 2). Kotter and Cohen (2002) continue by saying

> People rarely change through a rational process of analyze–think–change. They are much more likely to change in a see–feel–change sequence. Therefore, the leader must help people see new possibilities, hitting emotions and causing thoughtful processing that could affect behavior or beliefs. (p. 2)

Providing new experiences is one way to set the stage for groups to reexamine their beliefs.

This see–feel–change model can be applied to any professional development activity. The principal designs activities that create a common experience, have an emotional response, and guide conversations or study, staying true to our formula for school improvement.

The following four examples of context-building activities have real-life history of success. In fact, all examples in this book have been tried and used successfully.

Making Beliefs Visible:
Creating a License Plate or Slogan
(All-School Activity)

Purpose: The staff, in teams, will reconnect to their beliefs about children and education through reflection and discussion. Teams will create a license plate or slogan as a symbol of these beliefs, as did Carol Patterson's Explorer Team at Lake Oswego Junior High School:

Description: This all-school activity challenges faculty members to think seriously about their educational beliefs and the function and importance of teams, and leads them in examining their school's mission. Then, teams will turn those beliefs into a succinct slogan of five or six words, or a license plate that communicates to the larger community what those beliefs are.

Process: As a faculty, reread the school's vision or mission statement and goals. Review these; then discuss them in teams. Is the vision for the school consistent with your team's beliefs? Where is the intersection? What is missing? What might be added? In teams, do a quick write, individually addressing these questions. Share reflections and find common agreements. Can you prioritize these in an order that works for your team? If so, distill the first one or two into a short sentence that crystallizes your team's mission statement. As a group, condense these words even further. The end result should communicate what your team is about. Get creative, even silly; write, post, scribble, refine, and edit. Find something with punch that shares what you are about as a team. When you have it narrowed down to one to five words, what is your bottom line, who are you?

Materials needed: Scrap paper, posterboard, markers.

Debriefing questions: These can help guide the team in working through this activity.

- What is essential in our teamwork together?
- How do these ideas and beliefs relate directly to work with our students?
- Do we have a specific focus for this year?
- What would we go to the mat for? Is this reflected in our mission statement?
- Can we turn this into a slogan or catchphrase?
- Does this slogan or catchphrase tie directly to our work?

Follow-up: Ask teams to share their slogans or license plates at the end of the work time. Suggest that they live with their creation for a few weeks, then come back together to see what refinements are needed, if any. Once teams settle on their products, have them make posters. Post these in team rooms, halls, the faculty room, the entrance of the school, anywhere where others can see what you believe. Share them with students to underscore team identity. Use these license plates and slogans as titles for short articles in the school newsletter so that parents and others in the community understand what they mean and why they define your school.

Together We Make a Difference: Community Service
(All-School Activity with Students)

Purpose: If building a positive school climate is a priority, try using community service as the vehicle. To build value-added relationships, this activity brings faculty, students, parents, and local businesses together in mutually beneficial community service activities.

Description: This activity can easily become the annual, beginning-of-the-school-year, team relationship-building activity. Doing an all-school service activity brings the school in contact with parents and the community. Use time allotted for preplanning as service development time with faculty, setting the goals, structure, and procedures, and detailing all aspects of an off-site half- or full-day team-building experience. This time is critical to a successful experience.

Process: The key to doing any community service project is up-front planning and organization. Begin with a general staff discussion about the power of community service. As a start, agree on a structure for the school's activities and decide the time frame and the purpose of each activity. Communicate the educational purposes for each activity with students and their parents, the community, even the local school board. If you use teams as the community service structure, ask, "Where can we begin to make a visible difference as a school? Does our building need to be spiffed up? Are the grounds uninviting? What can we do with a little elbow grease that would be engaging and say, 'We live and learn together here.' What would make a difference?" One answer might be to paint the hall with colorful sayings and pictures. Paint and spruce up the faculty room or the restrooms. Weed the courtyard. Build raised garden beds and plant perennials. Pull ivy from a local natural area. Join a local service group on its community cleanup day, help a local business at a food bank, or assist a crew with Habitat for Humanity. Select a venue that fits with your team's curriculum or theme. Parents are great resources, with contacts to service clubs or local agencies. They can also link with bus services if student groups go off-site.

Now, determine how many parent chaperones you need, where each team will go, for how long, and what students will do. Design an off-campus parent permission slip and designate personnel to collect and tabulate these. Once sites are booked, make lists of materials needed: work gloves and garbage bags, cans of paint and cleanup materials if a painting project is your gig. Divide students into small groups, each monitored by an adult. Order bottles of water and snacks. On the day of the community service activity, use team time first thing in the morning to review the plans for the morning or the day, take roll, and finalize where each student group will be and who is in charge. Name tags and clipboards for student groups to record and reflect throughout the activity are good. When all activities have been completed and everyone is back on campus, bring the teams together to debrief. A quick write with three or four questions everyone completes is a good way to gather feedback and connect the activity to relationship building, themes, or key unit study questions. Celebrate jobs well done!

Materials needed: This depends, of course, on what activities are undertaken. Clipboards, paper and pens, name tags, paint, brushes, water cans, garden spades and shovels, garbage bags, bottles of water, snacks, thank-you notepaper, stamps, and the like may be needed. For any community service activity, time will be needed to make outside site contacts, to group students and make lists of who is going where and with whom, to contact parent volunteers, to order buses or get bus maps and tickets if using public transportation. Orient parents to your expectations for the experience and for student behavior. Have emergency contact lists available.

Debriefing questions:
- Why did we do this project?
- How did you feel about being part of the school and community in this way?
- Did you enjoy learning in this fashion? Why or why not?
- What did you learn about yourself and your teammates from this activity?

- What would you suggest we do differently to make this a more valuable learning experience?
- How did contributing to our larger community make you feel?
- If you could draw a picture or write a short story or poem about today, what might that look like? Sound like?

Follow-up: Don't forget to have teachers and parents debrief their activity together as well. What did they learn? What will they do differently next time to make this even more successful? What other supports do they need? Remember, everyone may be exhausted after a day of community service. Offer snacks to as you wrap up the day in a staff meeting. Ask parents for written feedback: what worked, what needs to be adjusted, would they help again? Ask the same questions to the off-site representative. Write thank-you notes to all who chaperoned groups and to the off-site representatives. Goodwill is imperative! Finally, ask that teachers find ways to tie new learning into lessons in the classroom. A journal-writing exercise, a science lab, a math activity, an art project, and a job shadow experience are all ways to keep the camaraderie alive and add value to the event. Take time during follow-up faculty and team meetings to share these or log the curriculum connections into team minutes for future reference.

Students and faculty join hands in a service learning project.

Navigating Obstacles and Taking Our Own Measure
(All-School Activity)

Purpose: If construction or remodeling is in progress, begin the year or new semester with this activity to create a positive mind-set when facing disruptions and inconvenience. Create a metaphor and have some fun as you help faculty develop a sense of order to cope with the disorder.

Description: Disruptions and major change can be irksome and impact the carefully laid plans of a school or team. When obstacles arise, help the faculty find ways to navigate around them constructively. Take this opportunity to build new context and connections. Find ways to laugh together and to see possibilities or solutions. From confusion look for "ahas" and clarity of mission and purpose.

Process: In the case of a major renovation or physical disruption to the facility, deliberately design an obstacle course in and around the school entry. Teachers coming to professional development meetings or back from vacation or a weekend can have fun climbing around, over, in, through, and past the barriers as they enter the building. Once inside, give each faculty member a small tool kit. Tools in this kit can symbolize important educational and school concepts, such as taking measure of ourselves (measuring tape), tightening our focus (tiny wrench), hammering in the essentials (tiny hammer), and balancing academics with relationship (small level). The Oriental Trading Company has many inexpensive props that can become symbols. An all-team activity might include designing team hard hats or creating a 3-D sculpture using recycled "found" objects. These fabulous artifacts can be displayed in a prominent place for others to enjoy.

Materials needed: For the obstacle course, use sawhorses, large empty boxes, ladders, safety tape, and netting. Hard hats or painter's hats, hot glue guns, "found" objects, arts and crafts supplies, cardboard, boards, wire, hammers, and nails are useful in creating "new" objects or wearable art. Purchase one small tool kit per staff member.

Debriefing questions:

- What is the connection between navigating obstacles and navigating learning?
- How do the tool kits create a mind-set for the year?
- How might you use your experiences today with students as school begins?
- How will you help students as you encounter and work around this disruption?
- What will you need as support over the next few months?

Follow-up: Teams can use the chaos and disruption to their advantage by teaching students to create metaphors about renovation, disruption, chaos, and change; sharing these with others in the school and community; and posting them on hall walls as a reminder that order will come from chaos. If rewiring or plumbing is underway, connect with the electricians, plumbers, and contractors to create science, electricity, or conduit labs and career exploration experiences. Ask teachers and teams to share how they connected the physical changes to their daily lessons and strategies for embracing the mess so others can expand upon this knowledge.

Accentuate the Positive with FISH!
and Japanese Fish Rubbings
(All-School Activity)

Purpose: This all-school activity will motivate the staff and help participants see their work as worthwhile in the face of mounting opposition.

Description: This activity highlights a company that found a way to add value to everything it does and pass that on to others. By viewing the FISH! video, four lessons will be uncovered. Each faculty member will identify one of the four lessons that resonates personally. Everyone makes a Japanese fish rubbing and adds his or her favorite saying onto the print. This art print will hang in the classroom as a daily reminder to share the spirit.

Process: You need to rent or purchase this video several weeks before you expect to show it. Preview it thoroughly. (To secure, contact Charthouse Learning at 1-800-328-2789.) Prior to showing this film to the faculty, ask each person to watch for the four lessons. Let staff members know they will be using this to underline their work the coming year. Then, watch the video together. Have everyone think quietly about the messages in the video, then pair the staff and share reflections. Ask that each person select the one lesson that really hit home to add to his or her fish print. Move to an uncarpeted area where tables and water are available. Bring out one fish per team (*yes, real fish*). The best fish for rubbings come from Japanese grocers. The grocer can help you choose which kinds of fish work best. Purchase fish in several sizes and shapes. If you purchase frozen fish, be sure to let them thaw out in an ice chest, without ice, prior to using. Remove the eyes before rubbing!

Directions for fish printmaking: Lay a fish out on newspapers. Cover the fish with a thin piece of paper. Using undiluted tempera paints, sponge paint on the paper over the fish. Add, mix, or layer color. Press hard enough to get scaled impressions. When finished, carefully remove the paper and let it dry. The next person follows the same procedure. After the rubbing is dry, use markers, ink pens, or calligraphy pens and add inspirational lessons alongside the fish print. When dry, hang these fish prints throughout the building or in classrooms as reminders of positive, optimistic attitudes.

Materials needed: Rent or purchase Charthouse Learning's FISH video. Purchase fresh fish for printmaking, tempera paints, brushes, sponges, calligraphy ink and pens or markers, newspapers, thin white paper 11 x 17" or larger.

Debriefing questions:

- What about this video impacted you personally?
- Which message resonates with you and why?
- Will what you saw make a difference in your day-to-day work with each other? with students? with parents?
- How will you make these mind-sets visible throughout the year?

Follow-up: This video is worth watching multiple times. Post FISH prints throughout the building. Refer back to the inspirational lessons and "throw" fish as you pass on that positive attitude!

3. Gaining Perspective—
Put Yourself in Their Shoes

D o your faculty remember how it feels to be a new student? It is important that staff members be mindful of the anxiety, fears, and excitement children face when starting middle school. Adults reliving the opening of school when they were students will remember what is important in middle level education (safety, relationships, an adult who knows and cares about you) and will work to allay those school jitters as they build relationships and forge team identity.

To recreate this sense of excitement tinged with anxiety, one Oregon middle school staff began the school year on the Willamette River. The principal arranged for the entire staff to take part in dragon boat racing. This was a new experience for most and provoked anxiety for many. The activity created the context or metaphor for the year. By learning to paddle together, to listen to the caller (leader), and stroke together, that faculty saw the power of working and learning something new together.

At the end of the time together on the water, reflection questions were posed:

- How did this experience parallel the first school day in September for an incoming or returning student?
- How did the experience underline the importance of building relationships and trust?
- What is the nature of communication as we change directions or meet individual needs?
- How does it feel when experiencing some new learning, such as using a paddle differently from using an oar? What implications does this have for teaching and learning and for building relationships in the classroom?

Feedback from the staff about the dragon boat adventure was consistent and positive; this experience built context for working together for student success with renewed understanding. To move forward and to make sure every student will succeed, begin by building on the power of strong relationships.

For some tasks, teamwork is necessary.

Enhancing Teamwork:
Dragon Boat Racing, Kayaking, or Canoeing
(All-School Activity)

Purpose: Sometimes to enhance teamwork and to see your work with students in a new light, it is necessary to change the context, get your group up and moving, and add the element of surprise to a professional development activity.

Description: When was the last time you moved into a new setting with new people, new expectations, or new learning and didn't feel anxious? This happens as school begins each year for new students. Will I find my classes? Can I open my locker? Who will eat lunch with me? Will anyone help me find my bus? This activity is the ultimate, out-of-the-box experience for bringing a group together. It builds context and teamwork, and bridges adult viewpoints with students' realities.

Process: Contact a local rowing club to see if Hong Kong racing boats or dragon boats are available in your area for rental, along with instructors. If they are, hire them! If not, find a local rowing club, a kayakers' group, or other on-water experience and check into what they can offer. Send a letter to the faculty prior to the week of professional development meetings, informing them to dress for an outdoor, context-building activity. Let them know they might get wet. Suggest everyone bring a change of clothes and a bottle of water. *Do not* tell anyone what the experience is. Remember, you are deliberately building a bit of anxiety! Do let your school director or central office official know what you are doing, when, and where, so you have district support. Arrange for a school bus to get everyone to the site. This keeps everyone together and adds to the suspense and camaraderie.

Once on site, introduce the activity and your guides, listen to instructions, don life jackets, and then board the boats. An experienced guide will have you practice paddling while teaching different strokes and the calls. If several boats are being used, have a race or two. If only one boat is available, do several timed sprints, using a variety of strokes, and total the times for each round. All activities lend themselves to conversation and reflection when back on dry land.

Debriefing questions:

- What can this experience tell us about working with each other?
- How does this experience relate to a student's first day in middle school?
- What can this experience tell us about working with all young adolescents?
- What did you learn about yourself today that you could take back to the classroom?
- What feelings did you experience that will help you next week with your students?

Follow-up: There will be a lot of excited and reflective conversation about this experience on the bus ride back to your school and in the days to follow. Anxiety of the unknown, the power of teamwork, and the connection to working with kids in new situations will surface. Find time in team meetings or faculty meetings to bring up the experience and reconnect the discussions to working with middle schoolers. Ask the faculty or teams to draw a picture or design a concept map of the activity as reminders of lessons learned. Post these in the faculty room or office as a visual reminder of the experience.

Special note

Is rowing on the river a bit too adventuresome or just inaccessible for your faculty and school? Try collaborating with a local high school or nearby college or sports facility and use a ropes course, cargo net, or rock-climbing wall as an alternative physical experience.

New Perspectives in Understanding: Compass Trust Walk
(All-School Activity)

Purpose: Leaders emerge when novel situations call for different skills. To rediscover who you are as individuals, as teams, and as leaders, this venture into unfamiliar territory creates opportunities and builds trust.

Description: This activity takes the faculty to an unfamiliar environment and requires that members trust one another as either a leader or a follower. This trust walk asks them to suspend criticism, work together for a common goal, assist each other, and discover individual and team strengths. These connections and insights enhance teams as they work to help students navigate learning and reach goals.

Process: Arrange to have a school bus available on the day of the activity. Prior to this activity, the principal must scope out a route that is unfamiliar to the faculty. A city park, a nature trail, city streets, and a set of college campus buildings, are all possible sites. Be creative and seek the unusual to add the unfamiliar to this activity. Be sure there are "obstacles" to maneuver. Walk the route selected and note four to eight landmarks that will become compass points. Chart the course on paper by compass points. Identify and list the key landmarks that correspond with all compass points. During the activity, each team's leader will identify the object or landmark that corresponds to each compass setting, such as a set of swings in a neighborhood park, a mailbox on a set of street corners, a particular subway station, a pin oak tree, and the like.

Notify staff prior to the activity day to come prepared by dressing casually with comfortable walking shoes. On activity day, have all participants board a school bus without knowing where they are going or what will happen there. Once on the bus, all participants don blindfolds. The blindfolds should be tightened as much as possible since they have to remain in place until the entire activity is completed. When the bus arrives at the drop-off site, ask for one volunteer per team. Do not answer questions about what the volunteer will do. Volunteers take off their blindfolds and are given a rope, a camera, a compass, and the set of compass points for the course. Volunteers must move the teams from point A to point B, and so on, taking a picture of the team at each compass point. The bus will meet the teams at the end of the course. They must get themselves to the bus by a certain time or be left behind.

Each lead person, often not the team's official leader, moves the still-blindfolded team off the bus using compass points. Some groups feel more confident holding on to a rope as they follow the course. Add an element of competition by adding time as a factor.

Materials needed: A bus to take the group members to the site and bring them back; one blindfold per participant; one compass, one long rope, one camera, and a site course map per team.

Debriefing questions:

- How did this activity relate to us? To our school?
- How did you feel donning the blindfold when you entered the bus?
- What gave you confidence to follow your leader?
- Did you anticipate the emotions you experienced?
- Could you have led the group?
- What would you have done differently?
- Did having the rope add a sense of security?
- How did you help your team?
- What strengths did you find in working as a team?
- How is this experience like starting middle school to a new student?

Follow-up: Often teams will refer back to this experience. In a faculty meeting, engage the faculty in a discussion about leadership and "followership," the role of team members, and the ideas of working as a unit: relate it to this experience. Follow up by asking how they will use these new insights and perspectives to navigate new coursework, address student issues, and offer a variety of leadership experiences to all students. Doing so keeps the ideas of leadership and "followership" alive and vital.

Working Together as a Team: Straw Power
(All-School Activity)

Purpose: To underscore a group's reliance on each other to be successful and to facilitate group effectiveness.

Description: The better a school or group of people works together, really listens, and supports each other in a variety of situations, the more the participants can laugh together and be available to each other. This short, low-stress activity asks all participants to listen, work together, and move physically into a variety of poses to achieve success for the whole group. After a long day, before moving into a meeting or beginning a professional development session, a good laugh works to open up and clear the mind. In this exercise participants bend and stretch, laugh, and act silly together.

Process: Ask the group to stand up and form a circle. Depending on the size of the group participating, two or more subgroups of 8–12 individuals may be needed. Give each person a drinking straw to hold in the right hand. Then instruct everyone to cross the right arm over the left arm in front of the chest. Position the straw between you and the person next to you so that you have a finger on one end of the straw and your neighbor has it by the left index fingertip. You hold the straw for your neighbor on your other side. Straws now connect everyone in the circle. Once in this position, attempt to do the following challenges together without dropping any straw connections.

- As a group, walk one complete rotation, and then reverse directions for another rotation.
- Move arms high and move arms low.
- Squat down to knee level and then rise up on the count of three.
- Form a square, a rectangle, a star.
- Sing a song in unison while doing a Rockettes kick.
- Make up other movements and ask the group to perform these while staying connected.

Materials needed: One straw per person.

Debriefing questions:

- Was this an easy task for you?
- Were the directions clear?
- Would better directions or better listening help?
- Who helped you if you were confused?
- Who took the leadership role?
- How effective were you as a group member?
- Were you frustrated at any point? Why or why not?
- What does this tell you about group membership?
- How does this relate to students? Do you let students help each other if they are confused about directions you give?

Follow-up: Suggest teams do this activity in classrooms whenever a group needs a physical demonstration of working together. It is also a great short physical activity to break up an extended teaching block as you move between learning modules.

4. Two Critical Components for Success

Having a common experience is an excellent beginning step to start the year and provides a context that correlates to one or both of the essential components of our formula. *Relationship building* is one key feature, and success for all students, *the achievement orientation,* is the other. By adding context through whole-group experiences, dynamic conversations and energy flow, building a base for focused, meaningful engagement. Remember, it takes the power of relationships with an achievement orientation to move a school forward.

Using the activity that follows, the conversations, ideas, questions, and input from key stakeholders can also provide direction as groups prioritize goals and design an action plan around the relationship-achievement equation.

Because my school's suburban area was changing from a sleepy, rural landscape to a bustling bedroom community with dense low-income housing alongside farms and mini-estates, I wanted the staff to move outside the school building and right into the lives of our students and their families. In order to change conversations and perspectives, I embraced the idea of opening the year with an activity that built context and created a yearlong focus for reflection and change. To start the new school year, my administrative team created a faculty car rally and scavenger hunt. Then, armed with new insights, the faculty and I grappled with the nature of our changing population and how we could change, adapt, or add programs and offerings to support student learning based on fluctuating demographics and student needs. After-school academic coaching, noon study halls, before-school library access supported by trained parent volunteers, and enrichment opportunities were additions that strengthened the school's culture for success.

Beyond Our Four Walls: A Car Rally and Scavenger Hunt
(All-School Activity)

Purpose: To expand the faculty's understanding of students' lives and to plan ways to more adequately meet the needs of a diverse student body.

Description: As communities change, students change. This activity propels the faculty into the community where the students and their families live and where the students spend their out-of-school time. The activity connects the adults from school to the community and expands awareness of resources, the dynamics of life in the community, and the obstacles that might impede student success.

Process: Prior to this half-day activity, the school's administrators must map out a route and identify 10 to 12 places where artifacts will be gathered. In a letter to staff, ask teams to organize vans or carpools for this opening professional development activity. Teams should ride together. At the beginning of the activity, tell the teams this scavenger hunt is a timed activity. Each group leader will receive a map and a packet with numbered envelopes. Each envelope, opened in sequence, holds clues to a site where an artifact is to be collected. Because this is a timed event, if all artifacts are not found by a certain time teams should return with what they have collected. The team that returns earliest with the most artifacts wins the grand prize. (Have in mind a wonderful grand prize—no bus duty for any week of their choice, one extra team assembly during the year—or something special.)

There are two rules: First, team leaders must open one envelope at a time in sequence. Second, teams must travel together to each location. Each clue leads to a place in the community that each team should see and where an artifact is waiting. Make sure the route covers your entire community. The envelope of clues and sites should give the faculty a view of the community, particularly its evolving nature. New developments should be included; areas that are no longer thriving but have become abandoned or boarded up should be considered. If students are bused long distances to school, make that part of the scavenger hunt. Send teams to both the most affluent and the poorest areas, to businesses, to local parks or natural areas, community centers, shopping centers, and athletic facilities. If the local chamber of commerce or other businesses are willing to participate, have officials greet the teams and explain what they do and how school-community links might be forged. Day care centers, senior centers, restaurants, and small businesses are often happy to develop new ties with the school.

Materials needed: Local maps; one packet per team with 10 to 12 envelopes containing clues and a list of artifacts to collect; one vehicle per team; prizes for the team with the most accurate artifact collection.

Debriefing questions:

- What did you learn about our community that was new to you?
- What has changed over the last 10 years? 5 years? 2 years?
- How does this affect the lives of our students?
- What difference will it or does it make in how you teach?
- Do we need to do things differently to support student learning and build a culture for success? If yes, what?
- Did you come across resources you might connect with this year to support students and your curriculum? What next steps will you put in place with these resources?

Follow-up: In a faculty or team meeting, direct the conversations beyond who collected what and who won the grand prize. What did the teams see that affect students, their academic success, their families' lives, and how we reach out to each one? Are there new or different connections teachers or teams will now make with our local community? How will these new understandings influence our work this year? Using this activity as a metaphor for the year will require continually recognizing the changes discovered and the impact they have on developing relationships to support each other, the community, and students. Ask each teacher and team to select one goal this year that builds on this experience and share that goal. Have progress reports regularly in team and faculty meetings. Check in during the year to keep the goal alive.

5. Leading Through Relationships

North Carolina's much revered basketball coach, Dean Smith (2004), has claimed, "The most important thing in good leadership is truly caring. . . . The best people in any profession care about the people they lead, and the people who are being led know when it's faked or not there at all" (p. 3-4).

As you enter a middle school in downtown Portland, Oregon, a large yellow sign hanging above the entry steps catches your eye. It reads

<u>Achievement • Balance • Relationships</u>
Excellence

The school's principal reminds us that most schools have a cooperative staff and team members who like each other, eat lunch together, and support each other. Implementing the relationship-achievement equation, however, takes more than caring. That's the message in the banner. To move the conversation up a notch so that teachers are sharing teaching practices and strategies together is risky, but it is the heart of true collaboration that supports excellence. It is that level of conversation, focused around teaching and learning, which comes about when relationships are strong and the focus is on rigor and on kids.

The following activity, designed to mine relationships, takes a faculty out of its usual comfort level and creates an infrastructure for the conversations around success for all that follow.

Out on a Limb: Low Ropes Challenge Course
(All-School Activity)

Purpose: To challenge everyone mentally and physically, deepen their trust in one another, and learn to work together.

Description: This activity puts people physically in unfamiliar and challenging situations where trust and mutual dependence are critical to success. For a team to be successful, every member must be successful. Many organizations use low ropes challenge courses as a way to teach collaboration by overcoming challenges and intentionally creating the conditions for each other's success. This activity allows teams to rediscover their strengths, take risks, and combine talents so everyone experiences success.

Process: Locate and contract with a local organization that has a low ropes challenge course (YMCA, college, neighborhood sports facility). Arrange for a bus for the day of the activity. Inform the staff that this activity will take place off campus, and that everyone needs to dress in comfortable clothes with closed toe walking shoes. Encourage each person to bring water. Arrange for someone to bring a camera. Order snacks. Arrange for a course leader or two to meet the group and take members through the various exercises. Announce the activity when the bus pulls up to the site. Let the group know the purpose of this activity—team building through meeting challenges—and that each should take on the challenges as he or she is comfortable and follow the course leader through exercises in pairs, mixed teams, or teams. Debrief over snacks and water before heading back to school.

Materials needed: Bottles of water, healthy snacks, and a camera.

Debriefing questions:

- What was your favorite or least favorite part of today's activity? Why?
- How did the experience today change what you thought or knew about yourself, your team, and your students?
- What did you learn today about yourself that you would take back with you to your team? To your classroom?

By joining hands, most tasks can be achieved.

As relationships are cemented, the school leader must move faculty conversation beyond knowing and liking each other to the achievement component equation so these conversations will relate to teaching practices. Honest conversations about teaching methods can tread on sacred ground. Peter Senge (1997) asserts

When you turn the mirror inward and learn to bring forward and scrutinize our practice, we make ourselves open to learning and growing. An effective leader understands this self-reflection stands on trusting and honest relationships aimed at helping students achieve. And when teams are truly learning, not only are they producing extraordinary results but the individual members are growing more rapidly than could have occurred otherwise. (p. 19)

Looking Critically at Ourselves: Hiking Mirror Lake
(All-School Activity)

Purpose: Reflection is a powerful metaphor. Ongoing reflection should be a priority in schools. This activity provides an opportunity for individual faculty members to look critically at themselves and their practices, recommit to teaching and learning, and bring reflection back into their repertoire.

Description: Take time to reflect on how we are doing. With thought-provoking questions and a quiet setting away from school, a half-day excursion can be the retreat everyone needs.

Process: Locate a serene setting within your area—a nature park with a pond or river, a retreat center, a grotto or environmental camp—that is available for a half day. Walk the site and identify three to six places where individuals can stop, sit, reflect, and write. Note, and perhaps mark, those areas. Arrange for a bus on the day of the activity. Compile a list of starter reflection questions, find a poem or two, or gather a collection of famous sayings that will provoke reflections on teaching and learning, the purpose of your work with students, balancing demands, and the like.

On the day of the activity, as members board the bus, give each person a small mirror tile, a notebook, and a pen or pencil. Provide team leaders with a set of guiding questions, poems and quotes, and other materials to share. Let teams know the purpose of the experience. Retreats are quiet, introspective experiences; and spots are available to sit and think. Let participants know that the area is also available for exploration. Encourage pairs or small groups to move off together and allow those who want to be alone to do so as well. Take time to look and listen to the sounds of silence, birds, and various outside noises; let your mind be still. Then, when you are ready, doodle, write about how you are doing in this moment, and reflect on the questions or inspirations shared. Set a time and a place to regroup.

Materials needed: Small ndividual mirror tiles, a bus, snacks and drinking water, journals, pens, and a list of reflection questions such as these:

- What personal goals did I set this year? Am I reaching them? What support do I need? What is getting in my way? Who on staff can help me grow?
- What has been the highlight of my year? What can I learn about myself as a practitioner from this?

Debriefing questions:

- On what did you reflect?
- Was this experience valuable to you? Why or why not?
- Where you able to distance yourself from your work and home life and still your mind?
- What part of today's experience will you take back to the classroom? To the team?
- What will it take to keep moving forward in terms of both relationships, adult to adult and adult to student? Did you have insights into your work with students?
- How will you use reflection in your own practice?
- How will you share your learning with students?
- Do you and your students use reflection as a common practice for goal setting and focus?

Follow up: Structure your return to school gently, as some will be deep into personal reflection. Quiet music on the bus or back on site, snacks, or a small gift validates the use of this time away. If possible, plan this activity when lunch can be provided for faculty when you return and the remainder of the day can be available to use in classrooms or as teams.

During the year, use your mirror tiles to make reflection a common occurrence, beginning or ending professional development activities with a thought-provoking question or quote, allowing time for teachers to write in their journals. Encourage teachers to use reflection with students regularly as well.

6. Sharing Leadership

An organization with an achievement orientation recognizes that success is attainable when leadership is shared. Shared leadership does not imply that the principal abdicates making decisions. Rather by expanding thoughtful, cooperative vision making and dynamic engagement at all levels of the organization, the principal is free to attend to administrative responsibilities, knowing that others will assume leadership in various activities. Collaborative leaders open the door for voices to be heard, broadening the base to share responsibility for school improvement and student success. When principals create a collective sense of responsibility, the attainment of school goals is accelerated. Additionally, the planning process can involve multiple faculty members.

Hargreaves (1997) emphasized the need for teachers to collaborate with each other with trust, candor, openness, risk taking, and commitment to continuous improvement.

Clark and Clark (2004) found that "to accomplish these functions, school leaders must engage their teachers in professional development strategies that support school-based, collaborative problem-solving and decision-making activities that are concentrated on improving student achievement" (p. 52). They also assert, "More democratic leadership increases the likelihood that teachers and other professionals will feel and be freer to engage in reflective practice and experimental learning" (p. 49).

By creating a culture that values and affirms different voices, by initiating a variety of activities and simulations, teacher leaders emerge. Anyone with knowledge and passion around an idea can bring that idea forward for serious consideration. That just might be the one idea that provides a breakthrough. When opening up the organization to sharing power, taking creative risks, and embracing the idea of trying something new with the end goal remaining steady—student achievement and personal success, a synergy often develops that can propel a group forward over roadblocks. Remember, sharing is dependent on the power of relationships.

The following activity helps groups grapple with the issue of autonomy versus central authority and mandates of the school administration, district, or the state. It highlights visually the need to trust each other's intentions and to find ways to think creatively if this important work is to be done collectively. Finally, this activity demonstrates that there is often more than one or two ways to accomplish complex goals while remaining faithful to set standards.

Teacher leaders emerge in collaborative activities.

Working with Mandates: A Creativity Exercise
(Leadership Team Activity)

Purpose: To find harmony among autonomy and imposed directives, mandates, and prescribed standards.

Description: On occasion, all of us have had to do something that we did not want to do. This activity is a metaphor for individuals and teams to be agile in their thinking while demonstrating the interrelated nature of autonomy and mandates. Introduce this activity by explaining how the all-school goals go hand in hand with team goals, and describe how creative instruction can work harmoniously with state mandates.

Process: Gather all materials prior to starting and place them in packets. Ask the team leaders to suspend judgments about the exercise and to follow the instructions in the packet you will give them. The instructions are as follows:

- Use the blue paper as background.
- Cut three shapes out of the green and three shapes out of the yellow. You choose the shapes and sizes.
- Glue your shapes to one side of the blue paper. Put your name on the back.
- Bring your creation to the next team leaders' meeting.

At the next meeting, share the creations. Finally, place a red dot precisely in the center of each creation. Stress this! The red dot symbolizes central authority, the expectations we must all meet. The shapes participants cut out represent the approaches and the creativity they bring to their work. Lead a discussion about the metaphor this activity symbolizes. Use concrete examples and listen as leaders delve deeper; insights into balance, autonomy, directives, and intentions will emerge. Refer back to the school's vision as the group wrestles with these ideas.

Materials needed: One glue stick and one packet per person with an instruction sheet; one sheet each of blue, green, and yellow paper; and a set of red circle dots.

Debriefing questions:

- What is your understanding of this activity as a metaphor?
- How does this exercise translate to your work as a teacher leader?
- Evaluate how you felt about the placement of the red dot. The red dot symbolizes district expectations, not choices.
  Did the red dot disturb your design?
- Can you use the red dot to see what is possible rather than what is not?
- How will you share this concept with your colleagues?
- How can you support this idea with your team?
- How might you use this exercise with your students?
- What lessons are inherent in the activity?

Follow-up: As you work together, refer to this activity and metaphor when issues of autonomy and central control or mandates are evident. "Remember the red dot" can become a mantra and bring a chuckle, reducing frustrations and tension when something new is added on the school's agenda. Keep the creations on display as a visual reminder of your connections to each other, the district, and the larger school community.

7. Nurturing Team Leaders

Effective teams provide a structure to check perspectives, build consensus, address conflict, facilitate problem solving, and move the leadership conversation—relationships and achievement—forward. When teams have leaders who are able to talk collaboratively about instruction, analyze test data together, share teaching strategies, make connections across subjects, and direct the discussion to reaching every student, then excellence is achievable. Working together and broadening the power base increase an organization's ability to adapt and change to meet student needs.

However, teachers do not automatically become effective team leaders. Professional development for leaders is essential to build capacity. Where do you start if the goal is to help team leaders hone their leadership skills?

Professional development experiences in some basic areas are required for school leadership teams to be effective. Topics would include

- The mechanics of adults' working together.
- The roles and responsibilities of a team or teacher leader.
- Ways to build consensus.
- Techniques for listening and communication.
- Models of decision making.
- The scope of their decision-making capacity when teacher-leaders represent a group of fellow professionals.
- Strategic planning and goal setting based on student data analysis.
- Systems or structures that facilitate ongoing professional development for teams to support curriculum and instruction.
- Supporting student advocacy models and activities.

A good place to start is with Branham's (1997) article, "Stephen Covey Comes to Middle School: The Seven Habits of Highly Effective Teams." The author analyzed and adapted Covey's seven habits of highly effective people. The seven habits, from thinking win-win to putting first things first, provide perspectives and strategies for team leaders as they work to build strong, functioning teams. Discussion of this article will bring many points to the surface and initiate needed reflection. The time invested to engage in these conversations about leadership helps team leaders develop their skills and pays off in both the larger school governance and team functioning.

Additional readings spark interesting dialogue. Look at recent best sellers in business to find new resource materials that support working in teams. Check out national conferences; professional development opportunities for leadership teams are plentiful. Reading research synopses, books, and professional literature, along with attending workshops, are all part of developing and sustaining strong team dynamics.

Promoting Dialogue and Skill Building
(Leadership Team Activity)

Purpose: To enhance teacher-leaders' capacity to work effectively with their colleagues.

Description: Effective team leaders do not just happen. Needed leadership skills can be learned, developed, and strengthened. Together, the administrator and team leaders identify requisite skills they want to focus on, from communication, leading meetings, conflict resolution, and motivating the reluctant teammate, to analyzing achievement data, goal setting, and moving a relationship-achievement agenda forward.

There is a large body of literature available about leadership and leadership styles. Organize short-term study groups with specific assignments and plans for groups to share the highlights of their reading with the larger group of team leaders and discuss the conclusions reached. Ultimately, the team leaders should agree on a few principles they will follow after dealing with the debriefing questions. The following set of readings is just a beginning. Use these resources as discussion starters. Share articles from professional organizations; contact state and national organizations for current research. Numerous conferences and workshops are available that target leadership development. Check out National Middle School Association's Summer Leadership Institutes at www.nmsa. org. Leadership Teams that meet together, learn, and solve problems together make for more effective schools in which all voices play a part. Remember, leadership development builds capacity!

Materials needed for initial readings:

- Donald T. Phillips, 1992, *Lincoln on leadership: Executive strategies for tough times.* His ideas about Lincoln's leadership abilities provide fodder for thoughtful conversation.
- Myla Goldberg, 2000, *The bee season.* Pages 1–8 help participants look at themselves in a different light.
- Wess Roberts, 1987, *The leadership secrets of Attila the Hun.* Chapters three and five especially, and pages 101–109 are worthy of consideration.

- Bob Deitel, February 2000, "Teamwork: Teaching partnerships pass the test," *Middle Ground*. Pages 10–14 raise pertinent teaming questions.
- Rick Wormeli, February 2000, "One teacher to another," *Middle Ground*. Pages 21–23 are good discussion starters.

Debriefing questions:

- Knowing where you are as a leader, what resonated with you?
- How does this play out in your work with your team?
- What did Lincoln or Attila teach you about working with a team of teachers? With students?
- How will leadership attributes from Branham's article influence your work as a team leader?
- What is working for you as a team leader, and where are the rough spots?
- Where do you envision needing additional leadership skills training as you move your team forward?

Follow-up: At each leadership meeting, start with some professional growth activity. Read an article together and discuss its implications. Bring up tough conversations and role-play non-threatening ways to approach them. Review current student achievement data and model analyzing the data. Lead the conversation to "How does this impact the way teaching occurs in our classrooms?" Show a video of a master teacher and analyze the teaching for effective strategies. Then suggest team leaders use or do the same with their teams.

Leadership teams must build frameworks and systems for ongoing work, taking time to engage in conversations, pose questions and ponder together, and build trusting relationships. Team leaders might consider doing the following activity with their teams to build context for their work together.

Melding Relationships and Achievement to Create a Shelter
(All-School Activity)

Purpose: To emphasize the power of teams when they work together to accomplish a goal.

Description: This activity asks teams to collaborate to reach a prescribed end by constructing a freestanding shelter, creatively using their problem-solving skills. Part of this activity occurs in silence.

Process: Prior to this activity, collect the five inches of newspapers and the masking tape and have them available in a large, open space. Gather participants in teams and present these rules: The entire team must be able to fit underneath the shelter. No one can hold up the shelter. All must play an active role in building the shelter. Teams have six minutes to plan strategies. During the planning, no one can touch any material and talking is allowed. After the six minutes, strategizing and construction begin; no one can talk. The construction must be completed in total silence. Teams have 20 minutes to complete their shelters.

Materials needed: Five inches of stacked newspaper and a roll of masking tape per team. Space!

Debriefing questions:

- What were some of the different strategies the groups used to complete this activity?
- What were some of the challenges you faced when the construction period began and no talking was allowed?
- How did the leadership and group problem-solving roles change?
- What aspect of this activity did you find most challenging?
- Looking back at this activity, what could your team have done differently to make this a more successful and productive activity?
- How will you use this new understanding of your team as you work together this year?

Follow-up: Use the debriefing conversations to have teams look at how they work together and how they solve problems. Ask that team leaders refer back to this activity as they approach obstacles and impasses as another way to see how they work together.

Listening to one another and hearing the message behind the spoken words are critical to moving the conversation into areas of teaching, learning, and strategies that support student success. The following activity highlights the impact of active listening and can be done as an entire faculty or in teams.

Teamwork and ingenuity resulted in an almost adequate shelter.

Who's Listening: Simultaneous Storytelling
(All Faculty or Team Activity)

Purpose: To highlight the power of active listening and underline the importance of listening to understand.

Description: In this powerful activity, your faculty will share stories in a venue that is less than optimal. Each faculty member tells a brief but important personal story to three other people. It is important that the story be heard and that the listener listen closely. When that does not happen, frustration is experienced. This lesson carries over to how we work with each other and how we listen to each other, our students, and their parents.

Process: At a faculty meeting or professional development activity, read or share your personal "why I became a teacher" story or "an obstacle I overcame" story to a small group. Remind your faculty that each of them has a story worth sharing. Allow four or five minutes for each individual to think through the story she or he will share with a small group. Divide the faculty into groups of four. Every member of every group will tell his or her story completely at the same time when told to begin, regardless of distractions.

When you see that everyone is ready, groups can begin sharing—
simultaneously!

When all members of the group have finished telling their stories, ask the following questions:

- How did you decide what story to tell?
- How did you feel as you anticipated sharing your story?
- Did you hope others would understand the importance of your story?
- How did you feel when you heard everyone was to tell his or her story at the same time? What did you learn from this experience?
- How will this experience affect how you work together as a team? With students in the classroom?

Materials needed: None.

Debriefing: Now, give participants time to really share stories with each other, one at a time.

Follow-up: Some faculty may become very frustrated during this exercise because the story they chose was very important and personal. Allow these feelings to surface and refer back to the experience so that staff members understand how important it is to be present and listen actively to others. The notion of "being present" is powerful and helps the speaker feel really listened to and understood. This is the effective communication we want to emulate in our work with each other.

Building strong, trusting relationships, where listening and understanding the intent of one's words is prevalent among the adults in the school, is crucial as teams address the second piece of our formula, the achievement orientation.

8. The Dynamics of Balance

The dynamics of schools rarely maintain the balance between building relationships and the achievement orientation. The effective middle school leader knows that the tension between the two dictates the amount of attention and resources to allocate and when one or the other takes precedent. The astute principal must continually assess the dynamics between relationships and achievement by narrowing or broadening the focus of the school's work, depending on which needs shoring up or what the data says is waning; by taking the students' "temperature" in the halls and lunchroom; and by being in tune with the school's leaders. Working on both relationships and an achievement orientation is critical for the organization's success.

In order to examine existing practices, the school must have a structure and a culture that recognize teachers as intellectuals rather than merely technicians (Little, 2003). Teachers and administrators must learn to talk together, critique ideas and practices, build rapport, and listen to and consider dissent. Marsh (2000) reminded us that reshaping the school involves planning backward from the intended results in a dynamic and powerful way that builds on the strengths of the school as a learning organization. He goes on to say that an organization must develop a shared understanding of the problem and redesign ways to address these problems to link learning and teaching practices.

The following two activities provide a look at two equally critical elements for success in the middle, cultural characteristics and program components.

Debating the Essentials for Effective Middle Level Schools
(All-School Activity)

Purpose: To increase awareness and reinforce understanding of essential middle school characteristics by using the two groups of characteristics presented in *This We Believe: Successful Schools for Young Adolescents* (National Middle School Association, 2003).

Description: Using the 14 elements of effective middle schools (p. 7), consider if one set is more influential or important than the other. Can your school be effective if only some of the characteristics are implemented? Why or why not? Can these 14 be ranked in any priority order? If yes, what order? These are important questions. Use a debate format; this lively interaction will engage the faculty and will broaden and deepen understanding of these critical elements.

Process: Let the faculty know that this activity is a debate and that everyone will play a part. Prepare a deck of playing cards, sorted with even numbers of red and black cards and one joker, and with the exact number of cards for the faculty members participating. Give each a playing card. Ask that no one switch cards. There are two debate teams: the Red Team and the Black Team. The person on each team with the highest-ranking card is the speaker or first debater; the person holding the lowest denomination is the team's coach. Remaining participants are researchers, note takers, or rebuttal experts. Whoever holds the joker is the timekeeper.

The Debate: Using *This We Believe: Successful Schools for Young Adolescents* as the primary resource, divide the 14 characteristics of effective middle schools into two parts; the first eight characteristics are the cultural elements, while characteristics 9 through 14 are program elements. The Red Team supports the cultural elements, while the Black Team supports the program elements. The debate involves each team's assertion that its essential elements are the more important set of elements for effective middle schools. Ask that each team put forth three to four points to support its point of view.

Timing: Each team has 30 minutes to prepare for the debate. Then, each debate speaker has a one-minute opening statement, followed by three minutes for supporting the assertion. Each debater or the rebuttal debater is allowed a one-minute counter argument. Following that, the coach has two minutes to work with the debater to create the closing statement. The Black Team begins the debate. The closing statements start with the Red Team, and the debate ends after the Black Team debater finishes his or her statement.

Materials needed: One deck of playing cards, a stopwatch, multiple copies of National Middle School Association's (2003) seminal position paper *This We Believe: Successful Schools for Young Adolescents,* and the list of 14 Essential Elements of Effective Middle Schools found in Appendix A.

Debriefing questions: The leader asks both teams to reflect back on the formula (relationships and an achievement orientation) and the 14 essential characteristics.

- Is there any alignment between these two? If so, describe them.
- Which elements need attention by your team?
- Is there a sense among your faculty that the 14 essential elements are all part of an integrated whole, or do some faculty members believe some characteristics carry more weight than others? How will this conversation move forward? Where are relationships and achievement on this continuum?
- Is it necessary to see "and" rather than "either/or" as you go about your business?
- What other "ands" are you faced with, and how have you connected those parts into a whole?

Follow-up: Often on a school faculty there is a sense that some elements are more important than others. The needed synergy occurs, however, when all 14 elements are in play. Ask that each teacher and team intentionally identify elements as they occur during the year as they engage in their work, and pinpoint ones that seemingly never come forward. Those should become individual, team, or school goals.

Balance: Who Wins? Individual, Team, and School Needs
(All-School Activity)

The thought-provoking, seven-minute DVD, *Balance*, a 1989 Academy Award Winner for Best Animated Short Film, can bring the relationship or achievement orientation dynamic into dramatic focus. It sets the stage for insightful conversations about knowledge, success for all students, enrichment, entitlement, shared leadership, and so much more.

Purpose: To illustrate the importance of working together by balancing individual needs and goals with those of the larger group. This big idea can take different forms, as this thought-provoking video will demonstrate.

Description: It takes a balancing act and a degree of selflessness to be part of a group while remaining true to your own needs and beliefs. This short DVD demonstrates in black and white what happens when balance is lost. As a reflective exercise, it will start conversation about what is important as you work together for success.

Process: Obtain a copy of the DVD. Preview it prior to showing it to the faculty (run time 7 minutes and 40 seconds). Ask that participants watch in silence and think about the concepts of power and balance. Give faculty paper and pencil. Immediately following the viewing, ask faculty to think about what message the DVD had for them and silently write in their journals for three to five minutes. Then pair staff to share their journaling (writing) and reactions. Allow for quiet conversations. Ask if anyone would be willing to share the pair's thoughts. Lead a conversation using the journal entries and debriefing questions.

Materials needed: The DVD, *Balance,* a short subject, is available from Spike and Mike's Cutting Edge Classics, Code DVDCEC, phone: 858.459.8707. Paper and pencils.

Debriefing questions:

- What did this film mean?
- What does it say about our work as a team, school, and community of learners?

- Where would you put relations and achievement on the plane?
- If the box were knowledge, does your interpretation change? Why or why not?
- What will you take away from this experience?
- Would you recommend this video to others? Why or why not?
- Could you use it with students? How? When? For what purpose?

Follow-up: This video can and should be seen several times over the space of a year as it evokes different feelings and understandings with each viewing.

9. Targeting Success

The second critical component of our winning formula is the achievement orientation that will lead to all students' achieving academically. The achievement orientation is met when there is a clear target in mind, when individuals and groups know the target, and when methods to assess performance against that target are defined. Once areas for improvement are recognized, then teaching and coaching become the crucial next steps.

In college basketball everyone knows the "target," to play well enough as individuals and as a team to win and then make it to the Final Four. That target is visible to all and orients practice. To play in the finals in college basketball's March Madness, winning teams and individual players must have a set of skills. Furthermore, the coach and team must share the larger understanding of where different skills fit into the team's game. They assess the team's strengths and coach to its weaknesses. They watch films of their play; they know the target and what they need to do to reach that target. When players develop a deep knowledge of how to play their game together, they have the flexibility to follow the game captain, to anticipate and react to the opponent. Synergy and momentum lend support to masterful execution.

In order for a school to increase student achievement, each person in the school must consciously focus on student progress, the achievement orientation. As coach, the principal recognizes the strengths of the school, the players, and what their skills and attitudes contribute to the whole. The principal models, cajoles, encourages, supports, and holds teachers accountable as they assess their own teaching strengths and attend to areas needing improvement. In the same manner, teachers and students analyze student strengths and learning needs. Once students know the target, what they are to learn, they are empowered to measure their progress and monitor what they need to learn and do to hit that target. When examples and exemplars are shown, when teaching strategies and content knowledge are meaningful, engaging, and congruent to the goals, learning occurs. New teachers and students must know what the target is, how they measure up against it, and how to get there. If the measure is short, teachers must have the skills and strategies to intercede and provide concentrated re-teaching to help individual students. Beyond the individual classroom, teachers and teams can coordinate content, concepts, and vocabulary to give larger perspective to learning, thus supporting each other and students. They can provide after-school help sessions. They can coordinate major tests and project due dates, communicate larger project time lines, and progress in meeting time lines to students and parents. In short, they can work together for success and academic achievement.

How might the principal create the context for targeting student success? The following activity will spotlight individual and group successes, pinpoint areas of need, and provide a professional development experience that is on target.

Hitting the Bull's-Eye: Zeroing In on Success
(All-School or Team Activity)

Purpose: For a faculty to define success as it relates to the school and their students and take a critical look at the supports in place to determine if these supports are adequate to do the job.

Description: This activity challenges the faculty to define the attributes of success in the school setting as they relate to student success, faculty success, and school success. Does success mean good grades or is success broader than that? For a teacher, does success mean students like you, or does it involve respect for how you help each student learn? These philosophical conversations lead to a deeper understanding of what is valued. From there, steer the focus of the conversations to identify what additional supports are needed to hit the bull's-eye.

Process: The exercise will take 60–90 minutes. Begin by asking all faculty members to write their own definitions of success. After a 60-second quick write, have participants share their definitions in pairs or triads. Ask the pairs or triads if any of their definitions would change if the target were student success, teacher success, school success. Ask table groups to agree on one definition of success. Have table groups write their definitions on chart paper and post them around the room. Following that discussion, group participants into grade level teams or curricular content teams. Each team gets a blank target with "Student Success" centered in the bull's-eye. Designate a recorder, a timekeeper, a presenter, and a runner. Using an agreed-upon definition of student success, label the various elements, conditions, programs, or supports in the concentric circles that lead to student success. After 20 minutes in teams, each presenter shares the group's bull's-eye. After all have shared, ask groups to note similarities and areas of disparity. These targets usually generate further discussion useful for identifying additional supports needed or selecting systems and structures that no longer work and need changing or eliminating.

If time allows, do the same exercise for teacher success. Define teacher success. Give teams another blank target and zero in on supports that lead to teacher success.

Materials needed: One or two blank targets (bull's-eye in concentric circles) per team.

Debriefing questions:

- What is your definition of student success?
- Do all students have to achieve success at the same time in the same way?
- How will you know when success is achieved?
- What data will you need to answer the three previous questions?
- What other information will you need to reach the bull's-eye? "I really need _____ to move in this direction."
- What support do you and your team or department need to meet the bull's-eye?

Follow-up: Have groups initial or sign their bull's-eye and post in the staff room or in team rooms. Invite participants to refine or rework these over the next week or two as ideas and words come to mind. After another week, review all concentric circles. If there are systems or supports one team has in place that others are interested in, share them. Refer to these bull's-eyes on a regular basis; the definition of success you've agreed on is valuable. Use the bull's-eye model with parents and students as well and let them define success. The end results might be surprising.

Allowing the entire teaching community to take part in the conversation about achievement is a formidable task and a real challenge. In addition to defining success, everyone must be clear about what is important, how it is measured, and how to analyze the data so they have meaning. Start by sharing your current collection of achievement data with your faculty by asking

- What do these measures and data sets mean for our school, for us as teachers, for our students?
- In analyzing academic achievement or other data, what is good enough?

- Who gets to analyze the data? Who makes the decisions about what the data say?
- What are students and parents saying about the school experience as seen through student and parent survey data?
- Where are students struggling? Succeeding?
- Which students are succeeding? Which are not?
- Do we have a broad array of scores that tell a full picture or is the data set narrow?
- What summative and formative assessments are needed to set targets for an achievement orientation? (Summative assessment is individual or group achievement as measured on standardized achievement tests. Formative assessments give students immediate feedback about themselves and support teacher diagnoses to respond to students' learning needs.)
- Do faculty members understand the difference between these two types of assessment and how they play out for students' academic growth?
- What training might you need to feel confident in your skills at analyzing data, reaching conclusions from the data, and crafting strategies to address deficiencies?

These questions are ones the Leadership Team or entire faculty should grapple with to pinpoint professional development needs for the upcoming year and beyond.

10. The Data Filter

When schools begin to gather data to look at where they are successful and where supports or changes in practice need to occur, the variety and comprehensiveness of data sets are usually slim. Annual standardized achievement scores, report card grades, attendance, and perhaps a parent or student survey are available. Certainly, there is information worth mining in these collections. Achievement data in disaggregated forms shape many conversations—and some practice. However, to move beyond traditional, school-wide data from longitudinal research of highly effective middle level schools is needed. To positively affect critical reading and math outcomes, high-functioning middle level schools embrace wholly the characteristics of *This We Believe: Successful Schools for Young Adolescents* (NMSA, 2003). National Middle School Association's (2005) *School Improvement Toolkit*, built on the 14 characteristics identified in *This We Believe*, will yield a broad array of data about the school beyond standardized test scores or local teacher assessment. The *Toolkit* guides educators in taking an objective look at multiple relevant data points. For more information and to view a descriptive video, visit www.nmsa.org/toolkit or call 1-800-528-NMSA.

The *School Improvement Toolkit* is comprehensive in nature, user friendly, rich in detail, and provides valuable insights. If needed, National Middle School Association will provide consultants to help you and your faculty interpret the data and develop a professional growth plan tailored to your school.

If your faculty needs a primer on using both summative assessment (large picture, program and curriculum) and formative assessment (individual progress towards goals), the Assessment Training Institute's *Assessment FOR Learning, An Action Guide for*

School Leaders (Chappuis, Stiggins, Arter, & Chappuis, 2004) is a terrific professional development tool. Additionally, Carol Stack's *A Passion for Proof* (2003) is a brief, excellent primer to use with an entire faculty. Look under Professional Development and Publications found on National Middle School Association's Web site for additional up-to-date, relevant resources (www.nmsa.org).

11. Mucking with Data

Armed with an array of assessment data and strategies for analysis, the Leadership Team can then begin to create structures for the faculty, to interact and reflect, and to muck around together with the numbers.

To build symbolic context for grappling with data, one school Leadership Team designed the following activity as the entrée for a professional development session on data analysis.

"Mucking around" became the metaphor. Gold horseshoes symbolized reflection and analysis, reminding the teams to interpret, not blame or accuse. The lessons of perspective garnered from a poetry performance helped another group see that analysis of the school's survey data was contextual.

Focusing on how to use the findings from the data is an important first step in an achievement orientation. These key questions help focus those conversations.

- How does a learning community promote higher achievement by all students?
- What are the barriers to improving student success?
- What are our criteria for high performance?
- How does our assessment information inform instruction?
- Noting some students are below standard, what mechanisms do we have in place for their support?
- What teaching and learning strategies and grouping practices best meet individual learning needs?
- How do we add this piece to regular planning?
- Do we have the skills and structures to make this happen?

When the target is student success, teaching and learning (the achievement orientation) become the heart of the conversation.

Creating a Symbol of Success: Golden Horseshoes
(All School Activity)

Purpose: To create an enduring symbol that is a metaphor for the complex task of analyzing and interpreting data.

Description: Take a big idea or complex concept; expose the small parts that make up the whole, and the invisible becomes visible. In this activity, faculty members clean old horseshoes by picking away at debris (think delving into and uncovering data points) to reveal the shiny horseshoe (golden nuggets that will lead to understanding why students had difficulty with a concept or particular content). Polish up your horseshoe to keep as a symbol of the importance of digging into the muck that is data to identify what is needed to help students be successful.

Process: This activity requires a bit of ingenuity. You need one horseshoe per faculty member. To get these discarded horseshoes, find a riding club, a horse farm, a stable, or a racetrack and make the call. On the day of the activity, take the faculty to a place outdoors where a mess can be made. Take the worn, muddy horseshoes you collected and give each person one to scrub and pick clean. Provide lots of soapy water, gloves, wire brushes, and metal picks. (Play some western music as people pick and scrub.) When horseshoes are clean and dry, spray paint each one gold. Tie a bit of raffia onto the horseshoe with a label that has the cleaner's name. Each person now has a symbol for the day's work: mucking around in the collection of raw data, picking, scraping, analyzing, and polishing what emerges.

Move into a faculty discussion about analyzing student data and relate it to picking and cleaning horseshoes. Ask team leaders to share the student data on hand within teams and begin looking for patterns, strengths, and shortcomings; draft consensus goals. How can you use this analysis to inform the teaching practices of individual teachers on the team and enhance student learning? Using the golden horseshoe as a paperweight is a symbolic way to remind each teacher of the work that went into poring over the data sets and finding golden nuggets to target.

Materials needed: One horseshoe per participant, picks, wire brushes, buckets of soapy water, paper towels, kitchen gloves, raffia, cans of gold spray paint, labels with names. Space to make a mess. Recent student achievement data by team. Paper and pencils.

Debriefing questions:

- Why start with dirty horseshoes?
- How does your horseshoe symbolize what you did here today?

Follow-up: Ask that teams set academic and student support goals based on the achievement data at hand. Develop and share action plans to reach those goals. Monitor progress at team and faculty meetings throughout the year.

Many schools have multiple data sets that include student achievement and behavioral data. However, different people can see the same data in different ways. One Leadership Team engaged teacher teams in the following context-building activity. What followed were rich conversations about achievement, perspective, success, and support.

Honoring Perspective Through Poetry Performance
(All-School Activity)

Purpose: To demonstrate that understanding varies as individuals derive meaning from different vantage points.

Description: Effective two-way communication cannot be taken for granted. Language can have multiple interpretations. This activity highlights the notion that our understanding of written or spoken communication is shaped by our backgrounds, prior experiences, and what we believe. Different interpretations do not mean one is necessarily right and others are wrong. Differences signify the need to dialogue, listen, and consider and that the speaker or writer think critically about the messages being conveyed and check to see what others understood the message to be.

Process: As an activity, choose one of the two poems provided in Appendix B. Divide the faculty into teams of four to five people. Give teams 30–45 minutes to read and decipher the poem and to create a performance that reflects their understanding of the poem. These performances will be shared with the faculty. All team members must take part in the team's performance.

After 45 minutes, reconvene the larger group and ask volunteers to start the performances. Allow time for each group to perform. Remember, interpretation is personal. Applause following every performance is always appreciated. Debrief the activity immediately following the final performance.

Materials needed: A copy of the poem selected, either "Naming of Parts" by Henry Reed or "A Ritual to Read to Each Other" by William Stafford, for each participant (see Appendix B).

Debriefing questions:

- How were the performances alike?
- Was the meaning changed by performances?
- Have seeing and hearing various interpretations lent deeper meaning to the poem for you?
- What relevance does this experience have for you at this time?
- How will it affect your work together?
- Can you use this activity with students?
- What outcome will you expect? Why?

Follow-up: Checking understanding and asking for clarification are important when working together. Use this poetry performance activity to model these communication skills and use them in your daily interactions.

12. Professional Learning Communities and Student Success

Effective teachers have a profound effect on student achievement. It is clear that improving students' academic performance is not possible without increasing the ability of teachers to engage students in high-quality instructional activities (Fullan, 2003; Jackson & Davis, 2000; Little, 2003; Marzano, 2003). In many schools, teaching is too often an isolated act. How does one create vehicles for conversation and collaboration among teachers so that walls then are broken down and sharing for student success is broadened beyond a single classroom? Jackson and Davis (2000) pointed out:

> For teachers, teams provide the kind of collaborative work group that is increasingly viewed as vital to organizational productivity across a wide range of professions. . . . Teams provide the essential mechanism for translating academic standards into engaging, interdisciplinary learning activities and assessment strategies that help young adolescents realize their full learning potential. . . . The ongoing dialogue of teachers on a team, especially when it is regularly focused on looking at student work to assess student learning and guide instructional strategies, is potentially the most powerful source of professional development for middle grades teachers. (p. 128)

The most promising forms of professional development engage teachers in thoughtfully and critically examining current practices in teacher study groups or in action research projects. They prepare teachers to employ techniques and perspectives of inquiry. To be sure, no one type of professional development is appropriate for all, but when the leadership team and the faculty "start small, think big," they can design professional development activities that make sense at the local level.

Professional development designed to meet specific local needs might look like this:

- A menu of seminars to support newer teachers with technical teacher skills (management, learn by doing seminars, teaching to concepts).
- Seasoned master teachers are given license to delve deeply into content knowledge and create rigorous and relevant learning for students.
- Small learning groups study middle school renewal and best practices, using National Middle School Association's (2005) *This We Believe in Action* and its companion DVD.
- A class on effective assessment for a small group of beginning teachers to use as a guide for professional growth for the year.

That is the target—to build and support professional learning communities that will impact the desired student achievement. Interaction is vital; through interactions, things are seen differently, choices appear, and needed actions are identified.

13. Leadership Keeps It Together

The effective school leader understands relationship building is key and is a consistent thread in establishing an environment where everyone is able to concentrate his or her energies and skills on student achievement. Relationships are critical to sustain teacher engagement in meaningful professional development activities around teaching and learning. Delving deeply into teaching and learning and student achievement is hard work. The preface from *Standards for School Leaders* (Interstate School Leaders Licensure Consortium, 1996) makes the following argument: "Effective school leaders are strong educators anchoring their work on central issues of learning and teaching and school improvement. Finally, they make strong connections with other people, valuing and caring for others as individuals and members of the educational community" (p. 99).

Newmann and Wehlage (1995) assert that school success can be defined as efforts that make a positive difference in student learning and performances, measured both by newer standards of performance and traditional achievement tests, where schools focus on teaching that requires students to think, to develop in-depth understanding, and to apply academic learning to important realistic problems. Schools, therefore, need to (1) learn to function as a professional community with a clear, common purpose for student learning, and (2) focus student learning and set standards for intellectual quality, sustained staff development, and more school autonomy (pp. 51–52).

Creating context through engaging experiences lays the foundation for nurturing strong relationships essential to re-framing the teaching and learning targets to find the most powerful ways to help students. Interdependence of people and ideas fosters local capacity. Using our formula as a guide, the critical attributes of relationships and an achievement orientation help keep a consistent focus, regardless of the many competing issues that bombard a school and faculty over the course of a year. It takes someone with time, vision, and hope to create and protect opportunities for staff to work together with common purpose. When our school was recognized as a school of distinction, I described the approach we used this way:

> It's like a child's kaleidoscope. Each rotation of the cylinder results in spinning and moving an array of colored glass pieces that eventually make a picture. When I work on building relations or move the conversation to students and achievement, I'm turning the cylinder. Different interactions bring different results; they all are part of the intricate workings of the kaleidoscope. The pieces of glass eventually fall into place and we have created a picture. Then, I rotate the cylinder another notch through another conversation or intentional experience, and we create again. It's complex and interactive; all the colored glass pieces are important and add to our picture. For me, the picture is being the best middle school we can be for our students. So I hold up the kaleidoscope and continue to rotate the cylinder, us, to create that colorful mosaic.

In the end, a school principal can design the context to underscore this formula: It takes the power of relationships with an achievement orientation to move a school forward. In such a school, collaboration and contemplation are keys, where colleagues are engaged in looking closely at student learning and refining their practice, and where success for all is not an afterthought.

References

Branham, L. (1997). Stephen Covey comes to middle school: The seven habits of highly effective teams. *Middle School Journal, 28*(5), 14–20.

Chappuis, S., Stiggins, J., Arter, J., & Chappuis, J. (2004). *Assessment for learning: An action guide for school leaders.* Portland, OR: Assessment Training Institute.

Carnegie Council on Adolescent Development. (1989). *Turning points: Preparing American youth for the 21st century.* New York: Carnegie Corporation of New York.

Clark, S. N., & Clark, D. C. (2004). Expert leadership and comprehensive professional development: A key to quality educators in middle schools. *Middle School Journal, 35*(4), 47–53.

Deitel, B. (2000). Teamwork: Teaching partnerships pass the test. *Middle Ground, 3*(4), 10–14.

Erb, T. (Ed.). (2005). *This we believe in action: Implementing successful middle schools.* Westerville, OH: National Middle School Association.

Felner, R. D., Kasak, D., Mulhall, P., & Flowers, N. (1997). The project on high performance learning communities: Applying the land-grant model to school reform. *Phi Delta Kappan, 78*(7), 520–531.

Fullan, M. (Ed.). (2003a). *The challenge of school change: A collection of articles.* Arlington Heights, IL: IRI/Skylight.

Fullan, M. (2003b). *The moral imperative of school leadership.* Thousand Oaks, CA: Ontario Principals' Council & Corwin Press.

Gladwell, M. (2000). *The tipping point: How little things can make a big difference.* Boston: Little, Brown.

Goldberg, M. (2000). *The bee season.* New York: Doubleday.

Hargreaves, A. (1997). Rethinking educational change: Going deeper and wider in the quest for success. In A. Hargreaves (Ed.), *Rethinking educational change with heart and mind: 1997 ASCD Yearbook* (pp. 1–26). Alexandria, VA: Association of Supervision and Curriculum Development.

Interstate School Leaders Licensure Consortium. (1996). *Standards for school leaders.* Washington, DC: Council of Chief State School Officers.

Jackson, A. W., & Davis, G. A. (2000). *Turning points 2000: Educating adolescents in the 21st century.* New York: Teachers College Press.

Kotter, J. & Cohen, D. (2002). *The heart of change.* Boston: Harvard Business School Press.

Little, J. W. (2003). Teachers professional development on a climate of educational reform. In M. Fullan (Ed.), *The challenge of school change* (pp. 137–180). Arlington Heights, IL: IRI/Skylight.

Marsh, D. D. (2000) Educational leadership for the twenty-first century: Integrating three essential perspectives. In Jossey-Bass (Ed.), *The Jossey-Bass reader on educational leadership* (pp. 126–145). San Francisco: Jossey-Bass.

Marzano, R. J. (2003). *What works in schools: Translating research into action.* Alexandria, VA: Association for Supervision and Curriculum Development.

National Middle School Association. (2003). *This we believe: Successful schools for young adolescents.* Westerville, OH: Author.

Newmann, F. M., & Wehlage, G. G. (1995). *Successful school restructuring: A report to the public and educators by the Center on Organization and Restructuring of Schools.* Washington, DC: American Federation of Teachers.

Phillips, D. T. (1992). *Lincoln on leadership: Executive strategies for tough times.* New York: Warner Books.

Reed, H. (1942). Naming of parts. *New Statesman and Nation, 24* (598), 92.

Roberts, W. (1987). *The leadership secrets of Attila the Hun.* Peregrine.

Senge, P. M. (1997). Give me a lever long enough . . . and single-handed I can move the world. In M. Fullan (Ed.), *The challenge of school change* (pp. 13–25). Arlington Heights, IL: IRI/Skylight.

Smith, D., & Bell, G. D. (2004). *The Carolina way: Leadership lessons from a life in coaching.* New York: The Penguin Press.

Stack, C. (2003). *A passion for proof: Using data to accelerate student achievement.* Westerville, OH: National Middle School Association.

Stafford, W. (1977). A ritual to read to each other. *Stories that could be true: New and collected poems.* New York: Harper and Row.

Wormeli, R. (2000). One teacher to another: Middle school teams, not in name only. *Middle Ground, 3*(4), 21–23.

Appendix A

National Middle School Association's
14 Characteristics of a Successful School

FOURTEEN ESSENTIAL ELEMENTS

Successful schools for young adolescents are characterized by a culture that includes

- Educators who value working with this age group and are prepared to do so
- Courageous, collaborative leadership
- A shared vision that guides decisions
- An inviting, supportive, and safe environment
- High expectations for every member of the learning community
- Students and teachers engaged in active learning
- An adult advocate for every student
- School-initiated family and community partnerships

Therefore, successful schools for young adolescents provide

- Curriculum that is relevant, challenging, integrative, and exploratory
- Multiple learning and teaching approaches that respond to their diversity
- Assessment and evaluation programs that promote quality learning
- Organizational structures that support meaningful relationships and learning
- School-wide efforts and policies that foster health, wellness, and safety
- Multifaceted guidance and support services

From *This We Believe: Successful Schools for Young Adolescents,* National Middle School Association, 2003, p. 7.

Appendix B

Poetry Performance Examples

Naming of Parts
by Henry Reed

Today we have naming of parts. Yesterday,
We had daily cleaning. And tomorrow morning,
We shall have what to do after firing. But today,
Today we have naming of parts. Japonica
Glistens like coral in all of the neighbouring gardens,
        And today we have naming of parts.

This is the lower sling swivel. And this
Is the upper sling swivel, whose use you will see,
When you are given your slings. And this is the piling swivel,
Which in your case you have not got. The branches
Hold in the gardens their silent, eloquent gestures,
        Which in our case we have not got.

This is the safety-catch, which is always released
With an easy flick of the thumb. And please do not let me
See anyone using his finger. You can do it quite easy
If you have any strength in your thumb. The blossoms
Are fragile and motionless, never letting anyone see
        Any of them using their finger.

And this you can see is the bolt. The purpose of this
Is to open the breech, as you see. We can slide it
Rapidly backwards and forwards: we call this
Easing the spring. And rapidly backwards and forwards
The early bees are assaulting and fumbling the flowers:
        They call it easing the Spring.

They call it easing the Spring: it is perfectly easy
If you have any strength in your thumb: like the bolt,
And the breech, and the cocking-piece, and the point of balance,
Which in our case we have not got; and the almond-blossom
Silent in all of the gardens and the bees going backwards and forwards,
        For today we have naming of parts.

A Ritual to Read to Each Other
by William Stafford

If you don't know the kind of person I am
And I don't know the kind of person you are
A pattern that others made may prevail in the world
And following the wrong god home we may miss our star.

For there is many a small betrayal in the mind,
A shrug that lets the fragile sequence break
Sending with shouts the horrible errors of childhood
Storming out to play through the broken dyke.

And as elephants parade holding each elephant's tail,
But if one wanders the circus won't find the park,
I call it cruel and maybe the root of all cruelty
To know what occurs but not recognize the fact.

And so I appeal to a voice, to something shadowy,
A remote important region in all who talk:
Though we could fool each other, we should consider
Lest the parade of our mutual life get lost in the dark.

For it is important that awake people be awake,
Or a breaking line may discourage them back to sleep;
The signals we give—yes or no, or maybe—
Should be clear: the darkness around us is deep.

About National Middle School Association

Since 1973, National Middle School Association (NMSA) has been the voice for those committed to the education and well-being of young adolescents and is the only national association dedicated exclusively to middle level youth.

NMSA's more than 30,000 members are principals, teachers, central office personnel, professors, college students, parents, community leaders, and educational consultants in the United States, Canada, and 46 other countries. A major advocacy of NMSA's is the recognition of October as Month of the Young Adolescent. This celebration engages a wide range of organizations to help schools, families, and communities celebrate and honor young adolescents for their contributions to society.

NMSA offers publications, professional development services, and events for middle level educators seeking to improve the education and overall development of 10- to 15-year-olds. In addition to the highly acclaimed *Middle School Journal, Middle Ground* magazine, and *Research in Middle Level Education Online*, we publish over 100 books on every facet of middle level education. Our landmark position paper, *This We Believe*, is recognized as the premier statement outlining the vision of middle level education.

Membership is open to anyone committed to the education of young adolescents. Visit www.nmsa.org or call 1-800-528-NMSA for more information.

Membership in
National Middle School Association

Become part of the only professional association devoted exclusively to excellence in education for young adolescents.

Access the best and most current research through *Middle School Journal*, our flagship publication, now in its 39th year. *Middle School Journal* leads the way in publishing research-based articles on middle level education policies, concepts, and practices. *Research in Middle Level Education Online* is a juried, Web-based publication focusing on current research in middle grades education.

Get great ideas in *Middle Ground* magazine, the leading publication for middle level practitioners. Each issue provides practical classroom and school-wide resources for teachers, teams, and school leaders.

Save time and benefit from 24/7 access to the best ideas, practical applications, and research. NMSA resources are at your fingertips on our Web site. As part of an institutional membership, an entire building staff has full member access to the NMSA Web site.

Stay up-to-date on trends and issues in middle level education with *Middle E-Connections*, our concise monthly update sent via e-mail.

Connect with your colleagues, stay current, share ideas and celebrate your profession at NMSA's Annual Conference, our Middle Level Essentials conference, or leadership institutes.

Customize a professional development program to fit your needs and your budget. Choose from our Annual Conference, Middle Level Essentials conference or leadership institutes, customized on-site professional development, Webinars and podcasts, and more than 150 publications. Receive substantial member discounts.

Grow professionally. An NMSA membership gives you access to support, information, and resources throughout your career.

Support your profession. Your membership supports NMSA efforts nationally and internationally as the leading advocate for young adolescents and middle level education.

Benefit from group discounts on professional liability and other insurance products, including identity theft protection, through our participation in the Trust for Insuring Educators (TIE).

NMSA.

For more information, visit **www.nmsa.org** or call **1-800-528-NMSA**.